IN MEMORY OF MY SON

MY STAR

Gail Sandford

Published by New Generation Publishing in 2020

First Edition

ISBN 978-1-80031-870-0

www.newgeneration-publishing.com

A MOTHER'S STORY OF GRIEF AND HOW TO SURVIVE

AN INTRODUCTION TO MY GRIEF I am not discounting dads and siblings, as they hurt too, but this is about how I got through.

What is a mum? Mums are not perfect, but they are special and wonderful: Mine was and I hope I have been and still am. Mums teach us how to be polite, to know right from wrong, to stand up for what we believe in, giving us strength to make wise decisions and to follow our dreams.

Mums nurture, encourage, and guide their children no matter where life takes you. Mums are here for you through the good and the bad, the happy and the sad.

We worry and panic wanting to know our children are safe; we want them to be happy and healthy and live a good life that is their own choice, making their own decisions as we all do.

Mums love unconditionally. We argue, we might even lose touch, but the best thing I ever did was have my two sons. I am so proud of my children.

One day you get a call and your whole life falls apart, but I will come back to my story in the next couple of chapters.

THE LOSS OF A LOVED ONE THROUGH A HOMICIDE

Shock and intense sorrow, helplessness, pain, distress, sadness, anger, numbness, loneliness. A big piece of you dies with your child.

You can't hold them, you can't see them –you can but not in the way you want too – you can't eat, can't sleep, you will hate it when people laugh and get on with life when you're going through so much pain. You want the world to stop; you want the nightmare to end. This will change you as a person from this day on. You will think and feel differently.

When you lose a child, as in my case a son through murder, all these feelings are intensified: a deeper level of shock, it's unexpected, a tragedy, unbelievable, and on top of all that it's a crime you have to deal with.

Your child's death is all over the media and you see it all the time, over and over again, and waiting for the person to be caught is heart breaking, devastating, in my case the murderer was caught, but what if they are never found? How do you find any peace?

Who did this to my son? Who is so evil and responsible? You want to kill the person who killed your child. This is so overwhelming you can't think straight, you can't understand, you can't believe this has happened. You will never make sense of it all. My feelings for the murderer are hate; he should suffer. I would like to kill him. I want him to die. I am not an uncaring or horrible person and would not hurt anyone, but now, through the worst thing that can happen in a mum's life, the loss of a child, I have an intense hatred for the person who killed my son.

My mum's mum was a lovely lady, a total sweetheart, lived into her nineties. My mum was as lovely as her mum, but unfortunately died before she should have. If my mum had been around when my son was murdered she would have known what to say and told me how to survive. I didn't have my mum, I didn't know what to do but I had to be strong for my other son, Stuart, who lives in the USA. Stuart was supported by two amazing people, Sharpe and Durk, who he lives with, his long-term friend Matthew from the UK, his wonderful friends Ruben and Jameson, plus many others he has made in the USA, and his counsellor from a non-profit organisation called LOVS. I cannot thank these people enough, thank you from the bottom of my heart.

I was supported by my long-term partner, sister Carol, brother Trevor, nephew Luke and my two friends Jayne and Alison who I have known for a very long time and seen my children grow up, my other great friends who I would not have known if I had not been with my partner. My son Paul, who was murdered, had amazing friends, more like a second family to him and they were a great support to me throughout all this. The family liaison officers and the police in charge of the case, the fantastic homicide victims support worker Rachael, my great counsellor Rob, along with the barrister and people at court, nurses from the hospital that looked after my son throughout his long-term renal illness.

Later on, two wonderful people, Claire and her colleague, helped me with my son's funeral, work colleagues and acquaintances, my doctor's receptionists, the wonderful nurse who had all the time in the world to just listen to me. Please understand how vital it is to have a good support network helping you through this, you can't do it alone. To everyone, you know who you are – I can't thank you enough. I would not have got to write my story if it was not for all of you.

MY SONS AND ME

My first-born Paul was thirty-eight years of age when he was murdered. He was a lovely baby. From a young age he developed renal failure, had a transplant which failed, and spent many years on dialysis looked after by wonderful doctors and nurses, who became friends to my son. He was so strong and courageous throughout his illness.

Don't get me wrong, he was no angel by any means, up to all sorts of things he shouldn't have. At times we did not speak for periods, and then we would be back in touch and close again. None of what he did stopped me from loving him and being proud of him. As a mum you want things to be different, but sometimes you cannot stop a person from doing as they choose to do. It hurts but nowhere near as the pain you feel when that child is no longer here, and has been murdered by an indescribable lowlife scum – words fail me, I can't find words to describe the person who took my precious child away from me.

My second son, Stuart, and my only child now, is forty-one years of age, is an artist in the USA and doing very well for himself, it must have been hard for him growing up as I devoted more time to his brother because of his illness. This was not intentional and I believe my son knows this as we are very close, again ups and downs, but he has grown into a very level-headed man. He is a strong person, but he had to be with all the pain and heart break plus trauma that were caused by his brother being murdered. He has been so strong for me and helped me throughout all of this while hurting himself. I am so very proud of the handsome man he has become, so loving and caring just like his brother was. He deserves the very best in life; he would make a great partner and a great dad. He has some great friends in the UK and the USA and they really care for him. He is an inspiration. My two sons, Paul and Stuart, are the best a mum could wish for.

ME

My name is Gail and I like to think I was a good mum and still am. It was not always easy but I raised two sons, so I think I got something right. I had my children young but would not turn back time, yes I have some regrets but not about having my son's.

My background is in care, looking after the elderly, working on psychiatric wards and supporting vulnerable adults and younger people who have ongoing mental health issues, supporting people in a care setting environment and the community. I just fell in to care but would not do anything else. I guess I just love to help people. I have helped my best friend Alison through cancer and been there for her. Thankfully she is doing brilliant and is cured. My other best friend Jayne has gone through depression, anxiety, panic attacks, marriage breakdown, unfounded accusations, and now she has something wrong in her heart but she will be okay. I am always there for my friends as they are for me.

My partner was diagnosed with an incurable illness this year, in hospital for weeks then discharged to be told he only has a few weeks to live. I decided no way was I losing someone else so I fought and encouraged him to live and he is continuing to do so. I have also recently passed a counselling course for working with people who suffer from anxiety. I want to pursue this avenue and I will, but first of all I want to help other mums going through the tragedy I have been through. In four years since my son Paul was taken away from me I have dealt with an awful lot. How did I do it? How did I survive? How did I get to where I am today?

CHAPTER 1

November 2015. The day after my birthday. I knew my son Paul had been attacked and was in hospital, but was looking at been discharged. We had spoken on my birthday, I never expected or even dreamed it was to be the last time I heard his voice or was able to tell him I loved him.

My worst nightmare was about to begin.

I was woken early in the morning with a phone call from my sister Carol, telling me Paul had died — no mum wants this call, but many have to suffer from senseless murders of their precious children.

I did not know how I felt, in fact I am not sure I felt anything as I was in shock and numb. I couldn't, didn't want to believe it – I had only spoken to Paul not more than fifteen hours ago. I had to pass the phone to my partner as I did not know how to react or even speak. You go through so much as a mum but this is the worst thing that can ever happen.

What do I do now, what did I do? I vaguely remember phoning Jayne, who said she would be with me as soon as she could get there. I sat at the kitchen table and cried like I had never cried before. I made more calls – who to I can't remember. How did I even call anybody? I was in shock; I was shaking, my heart breaking. Did I tell my other friend and other people? I don't recall.

All I could think of was having to wait eight hours before I could tell my son Stuart, who lives in America, which was excruciatingly painful. How do I tell him? What do I say?

He is too far away, I won't to be able to hold him and hug him, and it was so mind-numbingly awful.

My partner took over; he contacted the hospital and the police. The doctors believed a friend who was with my son was next of kin and I missed the opportunity to be with my son. I should have been with him or I should have been the first person to know but there was a mix up with the hospital and the police, but eventually it was sorted out and once again I thank the person for being with my son. It was few hours but seemed like a lifetime before two female officers arrived, they were to be my liaison officers, both really nice and supportive. My friend Jayne also arrived. I remember crying in her arms but the rest was a blur and still is blurry today as I write this. I will recall what I can.

The police were talking about murder, about a lowlife thug who attacked my son, and as a result of this my son's life was over and so was mine.

The police were with me a good few hours. I think asking questions and giving me information. How do you take it all in? It's impossible to even know what is been said. I wanted to see my son, my Paul, I wanted it not to be real and I had to find a way of being strong for his brother Stuart.

I remember the hugs from people and remember smoking endlessly and that's all I remember until later when Stuart did Skype from America.

I started to tell him but couldn't for crying, sobbing. My partner took over. All I wanted to do was hug my sons but I couldn't' one was in America and one was dead.

Stuart in America was looked after by two wonderful guys, Sharpe and Durk who he lived with and the amazing friends he had made. I am so grateful to these people, his second family, they are so lovely.

The police were here all the time, keeping me informed, as they had CCTV that had the murderer on film.

They did arrest someone but he was not the person responsible for taking my son's life.

I am not sure how my next few hours, days, weeks went, police, television, press, what the hell was going on.

I kept in constant touch with Stuart via Skype.

I went to see my son Paul; no mother should have to go through this. My friend Jayne came, I remember sitting waiting to see my precious child, I was numb and people talking, it was a blur, and the people were so lovely. I remember the lady told me she would look after my son and keep him safe, she was just being lovely.

I went in to see Paul with my friend holding my hand, I kissed and hugged my son and so did my friend, we promised him that the person who had done this would be punished, and I would look after his brother and continue to live for my son and do everything as an honour to him.

CHAPTER 2

Every time the TV was on it was on about my son, the person in charge of the case was giving a statement and pictures of my son were on television. I just wanted the person to be caught and punished and in some ways was glad that Stuart lived in America, so he didn't't have to see his brother Paul's face all the time.

I don't know how my son coped but with support from lovely people and constant updates from me, he was so strong and so supportive. I was trying to be strong for him but he was being this strong for me.

I went to see my son again and due to the nature of the situation – it being homicide – it was to be the last time I could go to see my beautiful son. I said my goodbyes and promised him once again I would be strong and survive.

Alison, when she came to see me brought me, some Red Door perfume. My son always used to buy me Red Door and now my friend continues to buy it in honour of Paul. My other friend Jayne also does this in honour of Paul. This is so thoughtful.

I kept getting updates from my family liaison officers: they had a few people they were questioning and also a couple who they were keeping in mind. I got up in the morning, I did all the things I was supposed to do, like wash my hair, get dressed and spoke to endless people. Friends of my son, who were like a second family to him, were so supportive and also suffering with his loss. It was unbelievable to all who knew my son and loved him.

Waiting for news unbearable, agonising, and painful, one minute I am sobbing the next I want to kill whoever did this to my son. I am so angry and hurt so much.

Through my family liaison officers I was introduced to a homicide support worker, Rachael. She was so caring and thoughtful, and helped me through so much. I remember a year or so later she got me some money from a charity so I could have a spa day with friends: a lovely gesture and a lovely day.

Along with police and the support worker, family, friends, things carried on. To me, though, I was in a bubble, on automatic pilot, getting through days and nights the best I could.

My support from the wonderful Rachael carried on for nearly two years; we had become friends and I needed her. I was able to talk about my son and anything and everything. She was lovely. My support was the best and I could not have got this far without it, I was asked if I wanted to see a counsellor, but at that time I didn't. I would know when the time would be right to see a counsellor and that time came after the funeral and court case, which was nearly a year later. I am wandering, so will get back to the story of the day they caught the person responsible for my son's murder.

CHAPTER 3

There was news that they may know who he was. People had given names to the police, people were talking.

I was told they had got this person. Did I feel relief? I suppose I did. Was I glad? Yes. Was I happy? No. This person didn't say much when questioned, but they knew, and thank God they detained him. It was found out he had done a runner after attacking my son and also got rid of his mobile phone, but thanks to the public and the great work from the police he was caught and was going to be punished.

It was going to be a long battle, a long time until the court case, but at least there would be some justice for my son and his family.

There was constant information, constant people around me. Don't get me wrong I am so very grateful, but sometimes you just need to be on your own to gather your thoughts and think about your loss.

I remember one day I needed the lovely caring nurse at my doctor's and phoned, spoke to the receptionist, and it just came out that my son had been murdered. They were very supportive and I apologised for just blurting it out.

They always made sure I got to see my GP or nurse anytime I wanted to. I got hugs and a lovely thing said to me, and was asked to keep them informed of everything. This was helpful.

The day came when he was locked up. It was a Saturday morning court, and I was so anxious until I got a call saying they were keeping him as it was murder and he would be locked up. It was a small weight off my mind.

It would go to trial and we would hopefully get a result.

It was strange to know a description of him, and it hurt so badly to know that someone could kill my child. I so would have liked to have got hold of him and beat him to death, but I would have been no better than him and I am so much better than him.

I would be patient and hope a trial would happen soon, but it will not happen until next year.

I made the decision to go back to work. I was a healthcare assistant and thought it would be an escape for my thoughts for a while... I didn't know how I would feel.

My employers were so lovely and so understanding, but as I was an agency worker I was not always in the same place so chose not to say anything.

The first few shifts were okay. I put on an act, did my job and went home.

I remember doing a good few nights – I would not sleep anyway so thought if I wore myself out with nights I might sleep better.

I ended up looking after someone who was end of life, but because I was on my own I somehow got through it.

Colleagues at work used to moan about everyday things. I wanted to scream and shout. They had nothing to moan about when I was going through hell. I wanted to shout my son has been murdered but kept quiet. Looking back I should have told everyone, but just thinking about it hurts so much.

I had to do a training day and with constant calls from the Police, I needed my phone on and needed to take calls. They were very sympathetic and I got through the day.

The days went on, police, work, family, I just carried on .I can't say I was living because I was in a bubble, a trance almost. The hours and days passed, but even though I looked okay –I took care of myself, went to work – nobody could see the pain inside me.

My heart was broken.

I started to tell a few close colleagues and they were wonderful and looked after me, they were supportive and caring.

CHAPTER 4

To quote from a song, "Time goes by so slowly", but it does go by, and you still feel you are in a bubble.

One day you get a call to say you can start arrangements for a funeral.

You're not supposed to be doing this, this is not real. You would never have believed just over six months later you were organising and having a funeral for your child.

How do you go about it? What do you do? Where to start?

I was put in touch with a wonderful lady, Claire, who was to become a good friend. She came out to see me. She was so nice, empathetic and caring.

A religious, sombre ceremony was not what I wanted – it had to celebrate my son Paul.

Ideas were discussed between my sister Carol, Stuart, the lovely Claire coordinating it, and myself. In fact, I did not have a clue. I don't think I said much but with help and support we eventually got somewhere.

I went back and forth with Stuart in America, telling each other our ideas. Also I spoke to my lost son's friends for ideas from them. I could not have done this without them.

It was eventually settled on a bespoke coffin of my Paul's liking. He loved cars, stars on top made from paper flowers for me, as he is my star.

A nice-looking car, music sorted to go in, out and in the middle, star balloons for letting off after, lemon curd tarts made by a close friend of my stolen son. He loved her lemon curd tarts.

The extended family of my son got photos together to show throughout. Thank you so much, for all you did. A sister of his best friend did great on the day and stood up and spoke about my son. The lovely celebrant said great thing about my son. A candle was lit for people to reflect and think about Paul.

The lovely person who organised it was with me from start to finish, family, friends, my other son, my son was so strong, his best friend supported him, and he supported me as did everybody.

Blue and pink were chosen colours, the date set. The weather was okay, it went like a dream, everything perfect, we even had a laugh at some photos and the song going out (Always look on the Bright side of life) – it was so very appropriate for my son. My best friend Jayne said a few beautiful words before we released the balloons and we all enjoyed a lemon curd tart or two. Thank you, Jayne, you were wonderful.

I am not sure if you had asked me the next day how it went as it was a bit of a blur, but as time goes by you remember more, how you got there, how you coped.

I chose along with Stuart to have Paul cremated, the wonderful lady who organised the funeral said she would keep my son with her until I was ready to scatter his ashes. What a lovely gesture –all you want sometimes is for somebody to do something nice for you and give you a great big hug.

We all gave him a good send off, we all did our very best, and all keep remembering my son.

It is the worst thing for a mum to do, but you can do it and can get through it. Be yourself, get support, be as strong as you can be and make your son proud.

He is my star in the sky.

CHAPTER 5

Time seems to just go on. I just continued functioning, going to work. I believe work really helped me, as a carer and not always in the same place I could go to work, pretend everything was alright then fall apart at home.

I was playing a waiting game as I knew before the year was out the court date would be set and the ordeal would begin for the person who is responsible for murdering my son.

One day I had a meeting with the police, who told me who the barrister and legal team were going to be, who would be supporting me in court, the date set for December.

The barrister for our side was highly recommended and well respected in his field. When I got to meet the legal team they were very supportive, very confident that the person who killed my son would be punished for the horrible crime he committed.

I was in contact with the legal team and was given information and a lot of support. It was going to be very painful and heart wrenching to see the person responsible and listen to everyone. I needed to attend court and would make myself strong enough to face the evil person.

I wanted justice for my son's death, wanted to see the person suffer.

The first day of court was looming. How would I be? How would I get through this?

I had a lot of support from my family, friends, police and legal team. Without my best friend and everybody I would not have even got to court.

Today was the first time I saw the person and his family. They were not suffering, they seemed cocky. I wanted them all to hurt.

The day passed, I held my nerves and kept myself from jumping over the balcony to kill the person on trial. I was told it would be a two-week trial. I do not know how I will do it but I will for my son.

I can't go into detail about the trial, but it was extremely upsetting, painful for me and all who loved him. I was exhausted, would go home, Skype Stuart, and relay it all. I was not able to sleep. I did eat as I was made to by support network.

It seemed to go on forever, but in reality it was a short court case.

The Legal teams had spoken, all witnesses had done their bit, the jury had listened, the judge had spoken now it was time for the jury to be dismissed and make a decision. Would it be murder or manslaughter?

The time had come. The jury came back. It was decided it was to be manslaughter. Murder would have been better but I could not do anything about it.

Before sentencing I had my letter read out. It was how I felt, what I thought of him and his family. Then he was sentenced to twelve years for the life of my son Paul.

Even if it had been double, triple it would never have been enough.

Glad it was over, as happy as I could be, the only thing is he can still see his family, talk to them. He is still alive; his family are not suffering.

I will always feel this way and believe every mum who has experienced or will experience what I have will feel the same.

Time to move forward, to live my life for my son.

CHAPTER 6

After all I have been through; I decided to see a counsellor. All the way through I had been in touch with a specialised counsellor and always knew if I really needed to talk to someone he was available.

I think with working in mental health for a number of years I thought I could work through it myself. I knew all the things I should be doing to look after my mental health: being kind to myself, eating, sleeping and socialising, talking about thing really helps. I think the main reason to see a counsellor for me was to channel my anger and hatred for the person who killed my son, changing it into something else. If I remained with this hatred it would have a negative effect on my well-being, I needed to let go of the anger and hatred so I could move on with my life. That's not to say I will ever stop wanting the person to hurt and suffer for the rest of his life, but I wanted to move forward for Paul and Stuart and for me, had a life to live and was going to live it.

I met with the Rob, my counsellor, several times. It was so good to talk about my son, along with everything and anything I wanted to talk about, I could say anything. I could shout, cry, scream and it really helped.

Putting yourself first is not being selfish, it helps and is so good for you and makes you feel better, it's good to be able to smile and laugh and be you again. It's good to reflect on things, to feel emotions and to let go, also to remember that your child would not want to see you ill or so miserable, so please be kind to yourself and get any help and support that is offered to you.

It has always been a dream of mine to be a counsellor, so maybe after all I have been through at a later date I will look into a course and maybe become a counsellor and help others.

CHAPTER 7

Over the past year and a half, on top of everything else I have already been through, I have supported two of my closest friends and my partner, although in hindsight I wish I had not supported my partner as he turned out to be a liar and a cheat, but that will be another story one day.

My friend Jayne of twenty years plus went through a break up and found it difficult to cope. On top of this she also went through a very emotional time, she suffered from anxiety, panic attacks and stress, she did have some counselling and it really helped. At the present time she has gone through a heart valve replacement and is doing well and I could not get through anything without her. I love her to bits.

My other friend, Alison, of fifty years plus ended up with breast cancer, had her operation, chemotherapy, radiotherapy and is doing really well. She was very anxious, I went with her to appointments and was with her when she had her operation, she still has anxieties and always will, but she is my brick and as with my other friend I could not get through without her. I love her to bits.

In early 2018, my partner was diagnosed with acute myeloid leukaemia, spent weeks in hospital with intense chemotherapy. I was having to work then visit. June 2018 he was discharged from hospital very weak and ill. I fought to get him back to good health, we managed a holiday in October then he started to deteriorate, nothing else could be done.

I gave up work to look after him until he passed away in February 2019, but he turned out to be a horrible liar and left me with nothing. But I will remain strong and move on again with my life.

While he was ill I managed to complete and pass with distinction a counselling course.

It's never easy when someone passes away, but nothing like your child being taken at the hands of someone. I just want to be able to help one mum who is hurting and going through the heartache and the tragedy I have been through.

CHAPTER 8

It's been five birthdays, three anniversaries of my son's funeral, and four anniversaries since the day my son Paul was murdered.

Time goes by quickly, but my heart does not heal and never will. I will always have a big gap in my life no matter where I go, what I do.

On the anniversaries of his murder I always buy blue star balloons and let them off into the sky. On Paul's birthdays I will have a certain food he liked, a burger and sweet potato fries, and a soft drink. On the anniversaries of his funeral I have a cup of tea and a lemon curd tart, these we had at the funeral. My son Paul loved a good lemon curd tart.

I have photos of my son in the house and I talk to him every single day. I am sure, knowing my son, he would be telling me to shut up, stop going on and on, but it's my way of feeling close to him.

Ever since the awful day I look at the sky at night and look for the brightest star, as that is my son. It gives me a lot of comfort.

It's lovely to celebrate these things with my family but if I can't then I will celebrate on my own.

At Christmas I always take care with decorating the tree, as this was one of my son's favourite things to do at Christmas, special baubles are hung on the tree for my son and his star goes on the top. In 2016 my other son was returning from Italy before going back to America. We decided for one anniversary at the beginning of the year to meet up in London and stay a few days to celebrate his brother and my son, also my other son's birthday was close by so it was a double celebration. It was special and I loved it.

It's so hard not being able to see your child on birthdays and Christmases, or being able to speak to them, but I still do these things and will always continue to do so. My way of coping, and every one of us who is so devastatingly unlucky to have lost a child at the hands of someone else, we have to cope the best way we can.

You never forget. You don't want to. Remember your child whatever way is best for you and celebrate their life.

Not long after my son had been tragically taken I had a tattoo: an Art Deco piece with a yellow star in the middle for my son, then later had a cat, a star, and my son's name on my arm. I went on to have a further tattoo but will let you know about that in another chapter.

I was so blessed to have my son for thirty-eight years, but wish it was a lot longer.

I love you my son and will never be the same without you.

CHAPTER 9

I continue to work and get on with my life, trying to enjoy every day. Still it's hard, you have constant reminders on the television or the radio, minute you will be okay the next you will feel sad. I try to smile more than cry, it's been a hard few years but I think I am coping quite well.

I work in care homes and other supported living projects, and looking after others is so rewarding.

I think I was put here on earth to care for people and will continue to do so.

I really want to be a counsellor and help others, but I will do when the time is right. Maybe after writing this book I may become an author that would be something. Both my sons, Paul and Stuart, would be so proud of me, as I have always been so proud of them both, and continue to be so proud of Stuart: he is a very talented artist and an amazing young man, as was his brother.

CHAPTER 10

Los Angeles, San Francisco, Palm Springs. To scatter my son's ashes. I wanted to do something wonderful for my Paul together with his brother Stuart. I wanted my son to be near his brother in America; until I got there it was not clear what we were going to do.

It was exciting planning my trip, also scary as I was taking my son's ashes and was travelling alone. But at the end of the journey my other son would be waiting for me and we would get to spend some quality time together.

I did not understand why my partner did not want to come with me, but I felt he did not really support me the way he should have.

Anyway, after my partner passed away he turned out to be a liar and cheat. Maybe I will write another book based on him, and I am so glad he did not come with me as it would have spoiled it all.

I am digressing now so will get back to my story.

I received my precious son's ashes and put them into an art deco bag I had bought specially to carry them in.

My flights and accommodation sorted, the day came to fly. Dropped off at the airport by my partner, I was a little nervous as I had my son with me and was not letting go until the time came when I needed to. I remember upsetting three airport staff as I had to tell them what was in my bag which in turn upset me. I got hugs from the airport staff.

I spoke to a lovely air steward on the plane who said if I liked he would put my precious package with his bag and would keep an eye on it. I agreed to this and settled down for my flight, excited, anxious, but happy to be seeing my son at the other end.

There were two flight attendants who kept coming to me to ask if I was okay and could they get me anything. These two lovely people helped my flight go by smoothly.

I arrived and had to go through customs. The person who dealt with me was very nice and wished me all the very best and told me to be happy as I could be, and that I was doing a wonderful thing for my son. I got my cases and could not wait to get to my son; we hugged for what seemed like ages, then we went on our way to my accommodation. I was so happy to be with my Stuart.

There was a mix up with keys at my accommodation, so I went to stay with my son at The Tom of Finland Foundation, his home in Echo Park. Sharp, and Durk, made me feel so welcome and as the weeks went by they couldn't do enough for me. I felt part of the family. Thank you for being in my Stuart's life.

We had planned some things to do, a baseball game, a tour of Paramount studio's, obviously Hollywood and lots more exciting things. I loved it. It was such a special time being with my son, his friends and family, just wonderful.

We went to Palm Springs had a great time, we went down there by a Tesla car and had what they call a pilot, he was so nice and we got on well. We also planned to go to San Francisco. We were thinking of things to do with our precious son and brother's ashes when we decided to do a plane scattering, ashes to be dropped over the Golden Gate Bridge this has meaning for my son and his brother to do with Star Wars.

We contacted the person who could do this for us and asked if possible to be done when we were in San Francisco; it was wonderful they said yes. I was to post my son's ashes and it would be all sorted. It was an anxious time as the ashes did not arrive when they should, but that was my son, he would do anything to cause may hem and cost money, even though he was no longer here. It also made us laugh as it was emotional but funny too.

Stressful for us both but eventually we got confirmation he had arrived and the scattering would take place as arranged. The stress seemed to flow away and we could relax a bit.

On the day of the scattering we went to Alcatraz, strange but very interesting, went shopping, then to the Golden Gate Bridge.

Amazing, as at the time we were on the Golden Gate Bridge a plane flew over and we both believed it was Paul. It was very emotional but also a relief to be able to do something wonderful together. He will now go all over the world and be with us when we need him.

We then decided to go and get commemorative tattoos. My son had some words that were special to him, "You are what you love", and I had a Forget-me-Not flower. We had a long day but it was truly worth every minute, it was the best, but sad and happy at the same time.

I love San Francisco and hope to go back many times.

Back to Los Angeles, enjoying the rest of our time together, what can I say, tinged with sadness but absolutely fabulous, as are both of my sons.

The time came for me to leave, I did not want to go home and if I had known about my partner I would have stayed in America.

It was sad to leave and be at home but I had to go back to work.

I had fantastic memories of my time in USA.

I can't believe that it was getting on to two years, time goes quick but we have to keep living for ourselves, the children we have lost, taken from us, and also live for the ones that are still with us.

Thank you to all the fabulous people I met in America.

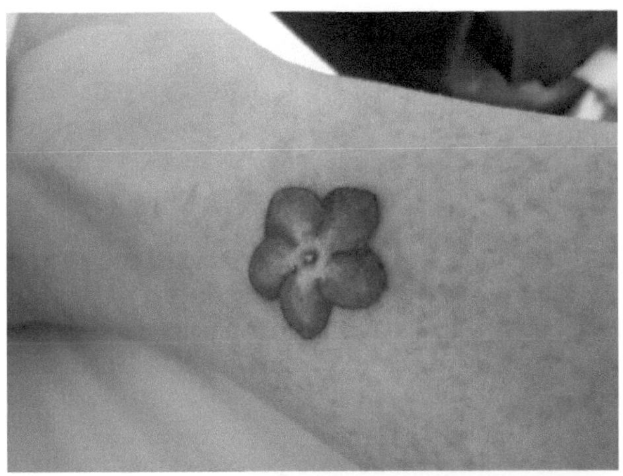

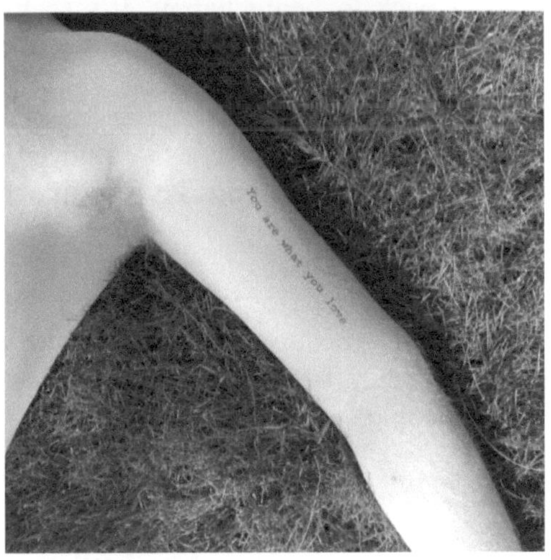

EPILOGUE

Life carries on. I think about my lost son every day and talk to my other son all the time. I have been blessed for having two wonderful sons and can't wait to see Stuart again. Hopefully I can go back to America soon.

As previously mentioned my partner became ill and passed away. Now I am doing my best to get that part of my life sorted again but I will. I have help from my family, my friends, my son in America, my son who was taken, and other great people.

I continue to look after vulnerable people, doing my best to get back to being happy. It's so hard but I am living proof that you can come back from the worst tragedy a mum has to suffer in her life.

Treasure what you have, as you never know when it could be taken away from you. Try and live the best life you can, and be happy.

Well, that is my story up to date. I really hope I can help any mums who are experiencing the loss of a child and hope one day I might be back with another book to help more people.

The End

A POEM FOR MY SON, PAUL

If I could turn back time you know I would.

To keep you safe, to protect you, to give you a big hug,

To tell you I love you just one more time, if only I could.

I didn't't get the chance to say goodbye and that will hurt for the rest of my life.

Whatever I do, wherever I go, I will always be thinking of you.

You were loved by many and will never be forgotten.

You were so strong, so brave.

My son. My star, shine bright and I will see you in the sky at night.

Good night, my son, sleep tight.

Love and miss you so much.

There are so many people to thank: my son Stuart, my family, my friends Jayne, Alison and many more, acquaintances, my lost son's family and friends, my son's family and friends in America. All the great people who helped me get to where I am today. A great big thank you to all of you, you know who you are.

About the Author

Gail Sandford has dedicated over 30 years of her life to looking after vulnerable adults in various care settings. She is a qualified anxiety counsellor and is working towards becoming a bereavement counsellor. She has a passion for dance and all things Art Deco.

My Star is her first book.

Email: gail.sandford@yahoo.co.uk

Instagram: @sandford1865

Twitter: @ellaellag

www.ingramcontent.com/pod-product-compliance
Ingram Content Group UK Ltd.
Pitfield, Milton Keynes, MK11 3LW, UK
UKHW042001190726
13854UKWH00005B/2109

9 781800 318700